This Is What I Want to Be

Truck Driver

Heather Miller

Heinemann Library

Chicago, Illinois

© 2003 Heinemann Library
a division of Reed Elsevier Inc.
Chicago, Illinois

Customer Service 888-454-2279
Visit our website at www.heinemannlibrary.com

Designed by Sue Emerson, Heineman Library; Page layout by Que-Net Media
Printed and bound in the United States by Lake Book Manufacturing, Inc.
Photo research by Alan Gottlieb

07 06 05 04 03
10 9 8 7 6 5 4 3 2 1

Library of Congress Cataloging-in-Publication Data
Miller, Heather.
  Truck driver / Heather Miller.
    v. cm. – (This is what I want to be)
Includes index.
Contents: What do truck drivers do? – What is a truck driver's day like? – What tools do truck drivers use? – Where do truck drivers work? – When do truck drivers work? – What kinds of truck drivers are there? – Are there other kinds of truck drivers? – What are some special things that truck drivers do? – How do people become truck drivers?
  ISBN 1-4034-0911-0 (HC), 1-4034-3608-8 (Pbk.)
  1. Truck driving–Vocational guidance–Juvenile literature. 2. Truck drivers–Juvenile literature. [1. Truck drivers. 2. Occupations.] I. Title.
  TL230.3 .M55 2003
  629.28'44'023–dc21

                    2002010294

Acknowledgments
The author and publishers are grateful to the following for permission to reproduce copyright material:
p. 4 Laima Druskis/Photo Researchers, Inc.; pp. 5, 10, 13, 14, 17, 18, 19, 20, 21 Bette Garber/Highway Images; p. 6 Bob Daemmrich/Stock Boston; p. 7 James A. Sugar/Corbis; pp. 8, 22R, 24 Walter Hodges/Getty Images; p. 9 David Frazier/Photo Researchers, Inc.; p. 11 Tom & Dee Ann McCarthy/Corbis; p. 12 Walter Hodges/Corbis; p. 15 Pablo Corral V/Corbis; p. 16 Gary Braasch/Corbis; pp. 22L, 24L David Frazier/Photo Researchers, Inc.; p. 23 (row 1, L-R) Bob Daemmrich/Stock Boston, Walter Hodges/Getty Images, Tom & Dee Ann McCarthy/Corbis, Bette Garber/Highway Images; (row 2, L-R) Siede Preis/Getty Images, Bette Garber/Highway Images, Bette Garber/Highway Images, Bette Garber/Highway Images; (row 3, L-R) Jeff Greenberg/Visuals Unlimited, Bette Garber/Highway Images, Walter Hodges/Getty Images, Bette Garber/Highway Images; (row 4) James A. Sugar/Corbis; p. 24a David Frazier/Photo Researchers, Inc.; back cover (L-R) Bette Garber/Highway Images, Tom & Dee Ann McCarthy/Corbis

Cover photograph by Bob Rowan/Progressive Image/Corbis

Every effort has been made to contact copyright holders of any material reproduced in this book. Any omissions will be rectified in subsequent printings if notice is given to the publisher.

Special thanks to our advisory panel for their help in the preparation of this book:
Alice Bethke, Library Consultant
Palo Alto, CA

Eileen Day, Preschool Teacher
Chicago, IL

Kathleen Gilbert,
Second Grade Teacher
Round Rock, TX

Sandra Gilbert,
Library Media Specialist
Fiest Elementary School
Houston, TX

Jan Gobeille, Kindergarten Teacher
Garfield Elementary
Oakland, CA

Angela Leeper,
Educational Consultant
North Carolina Department
of Public Instruction
Wake Forest, NC

We would also like to thank Devon Miller for his help in reviewing this book.

Some words are shown in bold, **like this.**
You can find them in the picture glossary on page 23.

Contents

What Do Truck Drivers Do?

Truck drivers drive trucks.

They take things from one place to another.

Some truck drivers take things around town.

Others take things to places far away.

What Is a Truck Driver's Day Like?

Truck drivers sometimes help load the trucks.

They must check their trucks before they make a trip.

Truck drivers stop to make **deliveries.**

They stop to pick up more **cargo.**

What Tools Do Truck Drivers Use?

dolly

ramp

Truck drivers load trucks with a **dolly**.

Ramps help them get into the back of big trucks.

computer

Truck drivers talk to people on **cell phones**.

They use special **computers** to keep track of **deliveries**.

Where Do Truck Drivers Work?

Some truck drivers travel on the **highway**.

They drive to places far away.

Other truck drivers work in neighborhoods like yours.

They bring **packages** to homes and stores.

When Do Truck Drivers Work?

Some truck drivers work during the day.

They go home at night.

Other truck drivers are on the road for days.

They stop to sleep in the **sleeper cab.**

What Kinds of Truck Drivers Are There?

Long-haul drivers drive long distances.

They drive big trucks, like this moving truck.

Some truck drivers deliver food.

This driver is making a **delivery** at a grocery store.

Are There Other Kinds of Truck Drivers?

Logging truck drivers haul logs.

The logs will be made into boards for houses.

Ice cream truck drivers sell treats!

What Special Things Do Truck Drivers Do?

scale

Truck drivers drive over **scales** to weigh their trucks.

The trucks must not be too heavy.

Truck drivers fill their trucks with **fuel.**

They use a **pump** to fill large **tanks** with fuel.

How Do People Become Truck Drivers?

Some people go to truck driving school to become truck drivers.

They study maps and traffic laws.

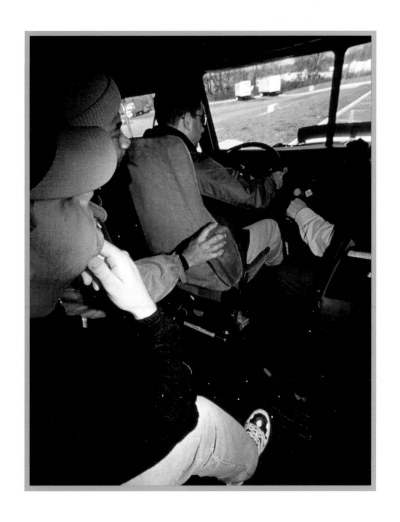

Truck drivers must practice driving.

They must pass a driving test.

Quiz

Can you remember what these things are called?

Look for the answers on page 24.

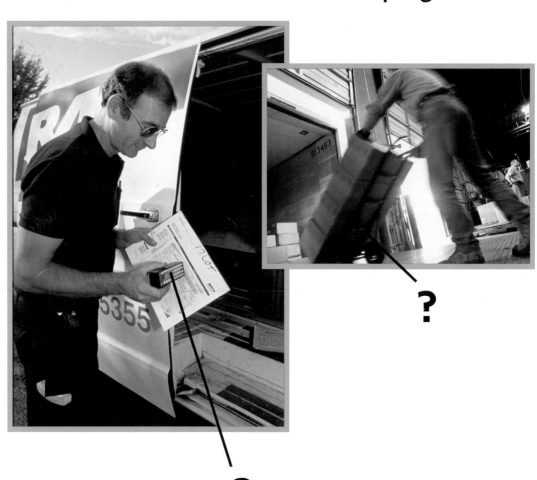

?

?

Picture Glossary

cargo
page 7

dolly
page 8

package
page 11

scale
page 18

cell phone
page 9

fuel
page 19

pump
page 19

sleeper cab
page 13

computer
page 9

highway
page 10

ramp
page 8

tank
page 19

delivery
pages 7, 9, 15

23

Note to Parents and Teachers

Reading for information is an important part of a child's literacy development. Learning begins with a question about something. Help children think of themselves as investigators and researchers by encouraging their questions about the world around them. Each chapter in this book begins with a question. Read the question together. Look at the pictures. Talk about what you think the answer might be. Then read the text to find out if your predictions were correct. Think of other questions you could ask about the topic, and discuss where you might find the answers. Assist children in using the picture glossary and the index to practice new vocabulary and research skills.

Index

Answers to quiz on page 22

computer   dolly